THE STORY OF THE
CHARLOTTE HORNETS

THE NBA:
A HISTORY
OF HOOPS

THE STORY OF THE
CHARLOTTE HORNETS

JIM WHITING

CREATIVE EDUCATION

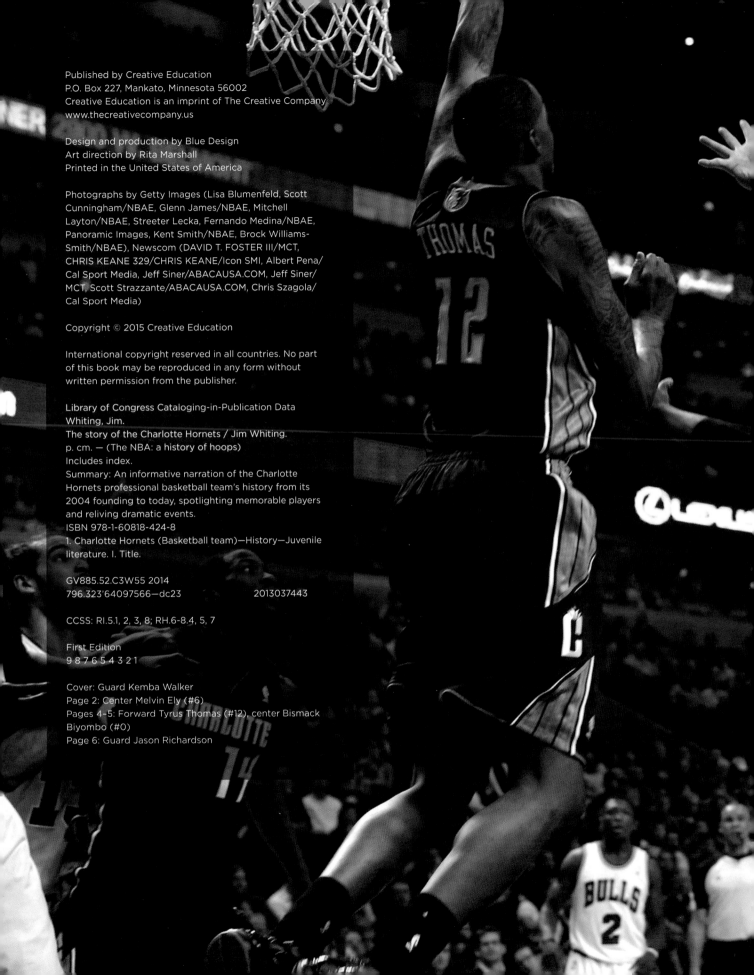

Published by Creative Education
P.O. Box 227, Mankato, Minnesota 56002
Creative Education is an imprint of The Creative Company
www.thecreativecompany.us

Design and production by Blue Design
Art direction by Rita Marshall
Printed in the United States of America

Photographs by Getty Images (Lisa Blumenfeld, Scott
Cunningham/NBAE, Glenn James/NBAE, Mitchell
Layton/NBAE, Streeter Lecka, Fernando Medina/NBAE,
Panoramic Images, Kent Smith/NBAE, Brock Williams-
Smith/NBAE), Newscom (DAVID T. FOSTER III/MCT,
CHRIS KEANE 329/CHRIS KEANE/Icon SMI, Albert Pena/
Cal Sport Media, Jeff Siner/ABACAUSA.COM, Jeff Siner/
MCT, Scott Strazzante/ABACAUSA.COM, Chris Szagola/
Cal Sport Media)

Library of Congress Cataloging-in-Publication Data
Whiting, Jim.
The story of the Charlotte Hornets / Jim Whiting.
p. cm. — (The NBA: a history of hoops)
Includes index.
Summary: An informative narration of the Charlotte
Hornets professional basketball team's history from its
2004 founding to today, spotlighting memorable players
and reliving dramatic events.
ISBN 978-1-60818-424-8
1. Charlotte Hornets (Basketball team)—History—Juvenile
literature. I. Title.

GV885.52.C3W55 2014
796.323'64097566—dc23   2013037443

CCSS: RI.5.1, 2, 3, 8; RH.6-8.4, 5, 7

First Edition
9 8 7 6 5 4 3 2 1

Cover: Guard Kemba Walker
Page 2: Center Melvin Ely (#6)
Pages 4–5: Forward Tyrus Thomas (#12), center Bismack
Biyombo (#0)
Page 6: Guard Jason Richardson

TABLE OF CONTENTS

COURTSIDE STORIES

INTRODUCING...

CHARLOTTE WELCOMES THE 'CATS

CHARLOTTE'S DOWNTOWN ARCHITECTURE HAS REFLECTED ITS PERIODS OF PROSPERITY IN BUSINESS.

The first white settlers arrived in the area of Charlotte, North Carolina, in 1755 and 13 years later named their community after the English King George III's wife. In the early 1800s, Charlotte became the site of the new American nation's first significant discovery of gold. North Carolina led the nation in production of the precious metal until the California Gold Rush of 1848. Today, gold of another sort—banking—is one of Charlotte's key industries, and the city trails only New York City as the United States' most important banking hub.

As a state, North Carolina is second to none in its enthusiasm for basketball. Especially noteworthy are two of the country's premier college basketball programs—the Duke University Blue Devils and the University of North Carolina Tar Heels. So it isn't surprising that the National

Basketball Association (NBA) announced on December 18, 2002, that Charlotte had been awarded a franchise.

The new team wasn't the city's first foray into the NBA. For 14 years, beginning in 1988, the city was home to the Charlotte Hornets. That team had a natural nickname. When British general Lord Charles Cornwallis occupied Charlotte—then little more than a village—during the Revolutionary War, stiff resistance from the local population caused him to label it "a hornet's nest," an image that is often used as the city's unofficial emblem. In May 2002, though, the Hornets moved to New Orleans, Louisiana. Hornets owners George Shinn and Ray Wooldridge claimed that dwindling attendance and playing in the outdated Charlotte Coliseum made it impossible for the franchise to compete financially with the league's other teams.

Despite the move, the NBA knew that Charlotte was still a great basketball city. So, just months after the Hornets departed, the league granted the city an expansion

ROBERT JOHNSON

TEAM OWNER
BOBCATS SEASONS
2004–10

Robert Johnson was a billionaire, but he started out far from wealthy. The 9th of 10 children, Johnson grew up in Freeport, Illinois, and worked hard at academics, studying history at the University of Illinois and getting a master's degree in international affairs at Princeton University. The Bobcats owner made his fortune by founding Black Entertainment Television (BET), a television network that focuses on the entertainment needs of African American viewers. Johnson turned his initial BET investment of $15,000 in 1979 into a $3-billion fortune over the span of 20 years. When he was awarded the Charlotte franchise in early 2003, he made history by becoming the first African American owner of a major professional sports franchise. "If you look at his background in terms of businesses he's in and has been in, it fits like a glove," said Jerry Colangelo, Phoenix Suns owner and head of the expansion committee. "The fact that he's an African American was a plus." In addition to the Bobcats, Johnson owned the Charlotte Sting franchise of the Women's NBA (WNBA) until the team folded in 2007.

THE BOBCATS' DEN

When Robert Johnson became owner of the expansion Bobcats, he knew his new team would be burdened with the same financial problems the Charlotte Hornets had had if it did not get a new arena. The Hornets' former home, the Charlotte Coliseum, was only 15 years old, but it lacked a major source of revenue: luxury box seating. In early 2003, Johnson received permission from the city to build a new arena in downtown Charlotte. "This facility will be state-of-the-art," Johnson promised at the arena's groundbreaking. "It will provide a premium entertainment experience for our fans." The Charlotte Bobcats Arena, completed in time for the start of the 2005–06 season, could hold 19,026 people and featured more than 60 luxury boxes. The arena also boasted a 36-foot-wide by 38-foot-tall, 80,000-pound Daktronic scoreboard. "The Daktronic display system is an important part of the building," said Barry Silberman, chief operating officer of the arena. "We wanted to provide fans with the ultimate 'wow' factor when they stepped into the seating bowl of the arena." In 2008, the arena's name was changed to the Time Warner Cable Arena to reflect new sponsorship.

> "WE'RE A BUNCH OF YOUNG GUYS WHO GOT OVERLOOKED. ALL YOU WANT IN THIS GAME IS A CHANCE TO SHOW THAT YOU CAN PLAY. THIS IS OUR CHANCE."
>
> — GERALD WALLACE ON HIS BOBCATS TEAMMATES

franchise. The newly created team's owner was businessman Robert Johnson, who became the first African American to own a major professional sports franchise.

The first order of business was naming the new team. During a six-month process, three finalists emerged: Bobcats, Dragons, and Flight. As Johnson explained in his announcement of the winner, "The Charlotte Bobcats team will be as athletic, fierce, and hard-working as the bobcat itself. No one wants to meet up with a bobcat in the woods, and that's the feeling we intend to create on the court with our team's new identity." The bobcat was also a natural feline complement to the Carolina Panthers, the city's professional football team.

ohnson hired Bernie Bickerstaff, who boasted more than 30 years of NBA experience, as head coach and general manager. "We want players who are young, inexpensive, and are gym rats," he explained. "We won't spend a bunch of money on older veterans who won't be around when we are ready to contend."

Bickerstaff plucked several promising players from the expansion draft, such as 7-foot-2 Slovenian center Primoz Brezec, sharpshooting guard Jason Kapono, and versatile forward Gerald Wallace. "We're a bunch of young guys who got overlooked," said Wallace. "All you want in this game is a chance to show that you can play. This is our chance."

Charlotte used the second overall pick of the 2004 NBA Draft to acquire University of Connecticut forward/center Emeka Okafor. "Emeka is a great player, but we see more than that in him," said Bickerstaff. "We are counting on his intelligence, strength, and maturity to pull this young team together." The Bobcats then added free agents Jason Hart (formerly with the San Antonio Spurs) and veteran Brevin Knight (from the Milwaukee Bucks) to share duties at point guard.

When the Bobcats officially entered the NBA as an expansion team, they needed a coach who could draw upon a deep well of experience to oversee the franchise's maturation. With nearly 30 years of NBA experience, Bernie Bickerstaff seemed an ideal choice to lead the team into its first season. "I love Bernie," said Miami Heat coach Pat Riley. "He's one of the best the NBA's ever had. He's one of the classiest guys around." Bickerstaff never pushed for the quick fix to get a few extra wins, instead favoring players who would jell with the team and young talent that would pan out in the long run. In his three years as head coach, he improved the Bobcats' win total each season, though they never got near the playoffs. "I always heard, 'you'll love him because he's respectful,'" said Bobcats guard Derek Anderson. "He sometimes swallows his pride just to get what he needs to get done for his team. A lot of coaches want the prime time. But it's obvious he doesn't care about that. He doesn't deviate from what he believes."

TAKING LOCAL TALENT

PRIMOZ BREZEC (#7) SCORED A CAREER-HIGH 13 POINTS PER GAME IN 2004–05.

T he NBA placed Charlotte in the Southeast Division of the Eastern Conference. On November 4, 2004, the Bobcats played their first game, squaring off against the Washington Wizards. Charlotte lost 103–96, but Bobcats fans got an early glimpse of what would be the team's strengths. Okafor and Brezec provided solid scoring punch and rebounding muscle, combining for 34 points and 19 boards; Knight directed the offense with a steady hand; and the whole team played tough defense. "Everybody said Charlotte was crazy because they went with all kids," said Houston Rockets coach Jeff Van Gundy. "But those kids fear no one and play their hearts out. They are only going to get better."

As is usually the case with expansion teams, the losses piled up. But there were highlights for Charlotte fans. On November 23, the Bobcats stunned the defending NBA

lay, Dec. 28th vs. Chicago. Ga

INTRODUCING...

EMEKA OKAFOR

POSITION FORWARD / CENTER
HEIGHT 6-FOOT-10
BOBCATS SEASONS
2004–09

Emeka Okafor was the Charlotte Bobcats' on-court leader and the face of the franchise almost from day one. Okafor was the first member of his family to be born in the United States, his parents both being natives of Nigeria. After growing up in Oklahoma and graduating from the University of Connecticut, he was selected in the first round of the 2004 NBA Draft. During his first season, Okafor used his go-to move, the jump hook, and his uncanny ability to rake in rebounds to rank first among all NBA rookies with 47 double-doubles in points and rebounds—an achievement that earned him the NBA's Rookie of the Year award. "I've had a pretty enjoyable experience," he said. "I can't complain at all. I've had a great time in Charlotte this year, and it's only going to get better." In the seasons that followed, Okafor proved himself a reliable workhorse, setting a franchise record by the 2007–08 season with 92 consecutive starts. In 2008–09, he ranked fourth in the NBA in rebounds and ninth in blocked shots. He was then traded to New Orleans in 2009 and joined the Washington Wizards in 2012.

champion Detroit Pistons, 91–89. They became the first expansion team since 1971 to beat a reigning NBA champ.

The Bobcats put together another notable performance on December 14, when the New Orleans Hornets—Charlotte's old club—came to town. The Bobcats organization called it "Conversion Night," allowing fans to trade old Hornets apparel for a free orange Bobcats hat. With five seconds left in overtime, Okafor sank two free throws for a 94–93 triumph. "Any win is important for us, but this one, you could just sense the fans wanted it," said Okafor. "They wanted us to beat the Hornets, and we sensed it meant a lot to the city."

Charlotte finished its first season with a mark of 18–64, the same record as New Orleans. Okafor showed his star potential by posting double-digit totals in points and rebounds in 19 straight games—the longest "double-double" streak by an NBA rookie in 36 years—and was voted Rookie of the Year. Brezec and Wallace emerged as solid starters, and Knight's nine assists per game ranked second-best in the entire league.

In the 2005 NBA Draft, the Bobcats chose two University of North Carolina stars, forward Sean May and point guard Raymond Felton. The burly May and speedy Felton had led the Tar Heels to the 2005 college national championship and seemed sure bets to boost the Bobcats.

Four months later, the Bobcats' new home, the Charlotte Bobcats Arena, opened its doors. In the first game, the Bobcats trailed the Boston Celtics by 10 points with 3 minutes to go before roaring back and sending the game into

overtime. In the extra period, Wallace drilled a long jump shot for a 107–105 win. On November 16, the Bobcats crushed the Pacers 122–90 for the most lopsided victory in team history.

Unfortunately, the season turned sour when May and Okafor were lost for the year with injuries. Wallace sat out a third of the season with injured ribs. But Charlotte refused to quit, rallying behind the inspired play of Felton and forward Jumaine Jones. Felton put his great court vision and incredible quickness on display all season, earning three NBA Rookie of the Month awards. Jones, acquired in a preseason trade, gave the Bobcats steady scoring and veteran leadership.

Other players stepped up for the Bobcats late in the season. On April 17, rookie guard Alan Anderson notched a career-high 18 points in a 98–91 win over the New York Knicks. Center Jake Voskuhl also added 17 points in that game, including a key outside jumper in the third quarter that gave the Bobcats the lead for good. Two nights later, in the last game of the season, guard Matt Carroll and center Melvin Ely combined for 42 points in a 96–86 Bobcats win over the Philadelphia 76ers. Thanks to such efforts, Charlotte finished the season with four consecutive wins—the most in franchise history. "Considering what we did, finishing with 26 wins and a 4-game win streak, despite the injuries, we can count this as an excellent season," Wallace said.

WIN NUMBER ONE

It didn't take long for the Charlotte Bobcats to notch their first victory. In the second game of the 2004–05 season, the Bobcats out-hustled the Orlando Magic en route to a stirring 111–100 victory in front of 20,873 Bobcats fans in the Charlotte Coliseum. Swingman Gerald Wallace poured in 18 points, including 2 in the third quarter when he took an alley-oop pass from guard Jason Hart and slammed it home in a highlight that roused the crowd. "I tried to come out and give it my all," said Wallace. "I just laid my body on the line and did what I had to do to help my team win." The game also marked the first of what promised to be many great head-to-head duels between the first two picks of the 2004 NBA Draft: Orlando forward/center Dwight Howard and Bobcats forward/center Emeka Okafor. Like his team, Okafor won the battle that night, scoring 12 points while holding Howard to 5. "That," predicted Bobcats coach and general manager Bernie Bickerstaff, "will be a great matchup for the next 15 years."

MJ MOVES IN

IN 2005–06, HIS SOLE SEASON IN CHARLOTTE, JUMAINE JONES CONTRIBUTED 799 POINTS.

In the off-season, the team got more good news when Michael Jordan, arguably the greatest player of all time, was named part-owner of the Bobcats. Jordan, a North Carolina native, became manager of basketball operations, which put him in charge of picking the franchise's players and coaches. With this sports icon on board, the Bobcats' prospects looked even brighter.

Even though the Bobcats had added Jordan's sports savvy and celebrity, the young team needed another "go-to" player if it was going to continue to improve. One of Jordan's first decisions was to use the club's top pick in the 2006 NBA Draft for sweet-shooting Gonzaga University forward Adam Morrison. "Adam is a clever and creative player who is a proven scorer," said Bickerstaff. "We really like the way Adam competes—he is one of the most competitive players I have seen—and that mentality

STAR OWNERS

In addition to majority owner Robert Johnson, the Charlotte Bobcats have featured an impressive list of high-profile part-owners, such as former NBA player M. L. Carr and NASCAR racing team owner Felix Sabates. Also joining the team in an ownership capacity was Cornell "Nelly" Haynes Jr., a Grammy Award-winning rapper and movie actor who became a minority owner of the Bobcats franchise in the summer of 2004. "To be able to make this move with majority owner Robert Johnson, and to be part of the first ever minority-owned professional sports franchise in history is a great opportunity," he said. But the most notable of the celebrities was one of the world's most popular NBA figures, Michael Jordan. Jordan, a native of North Carolina, joined the club in 2006, acting as the team's managing member of basketball operations. "He's known as the best player in the game—he'll be a big asset to this team," said guard Raymond Felton. In 2010, Johnson sold majority ownership of the franchise to Jordan.

fits in with the team we have." The Bobcats also added center Ryan Hollins, a shot-blocking sensation from the University of California, Los Angeles (UCLA), with their second-round pick and signed forward Walter Herrmann, a 6-foot-9 Argentinean who had a reputation for toughness and intensity.

The Bobcats lost the first two games of the 2006–07 season, and with superstar forward LeBron James and the Cleveland Cavaliers coming to town for the third game, it seemed likely Charlotte would go 0–3. But the Bobcats fought the Cavaliers to a virtual stalemate and

eked out a satisfying 92–88 win. "I guess we killed two birds with one stone—got our first victory of the season and our first win against Cleveland—and it feels great," Okafor said.

Unfortunately, that flash of brilliance was the exception rather than the trend for Charlotte, as the club would start the season a dismal 7–21. By the middle of December, the Bobcats needed a spark, and they got it from several different players as they racked up some impressive victories. On December 14, May used his soft shooting touch down low to net a career-high 32 points in a 99–89 victory over

LOYAL BOBCATS FANS DID NOT ALLOW A STRING OF LOSING RECORDS TO DAMPEN THEIR ENTHUSIASM.

INTRODUCING...

GERALD WALLACE

POSITION FORWARD
HEIGHT 6-FOOT-7
BOBCATS SEASONS
2004–11

Gerald Wallace could do it all. A forward with an array of talents, he could actually play three positions: small forward, power forward, and shooting guard. Wallace went pro in 2001 after only one season at the University of Alabama, being selected in the first round by the Sacramento Kings. Wallace spent most of his time in Sacramento on the bench, but in 2004, the Bobcats acquired him in the expansion draft. Given the chance to play, Wallace proved himself to be a relentless defender and a top-tier scoring threat, earning the nickname "G-Force" from his teammates. "One of the first things I wanted to do when I first came into the NBA was work on my defense," Wallace said. "Anybody can score 30 to 40 points a game, but can you stop a guy from scoring 30 to 40 points? That's what separates the great guys from the best in the world." His spirited play and willingness caused him to suffer frequent injuries, but he remained a key spark plug in the Bobcats' offense until he was traded to the Portland Trail Blazers in 2011.

"HE'S FROM NORTH CAROLINA. HE WENT TO THE UNIVERSITY OF NORTH CAROLINA, HAS FAMILY HERE. HE'S LOOKING FORWARD TO COMING BACK, AND I'M VERY HAPPY I COULD BRING HIM BACK."

— MICHAEL JORDAN ON COACH LARRY BROWN

the Magic. On December 29, Okafor showcased his multidimensional game by grabbing a career-high 25 rebounds and scoring 22 points to help topple the Los Angeles Lakers. Wallace made team history on January 31, pouring in a then franchise-record 42 points in a win over the Knicks. "That's phenomenal," said Bobcats guard Derek Anderson. "We found a guy and we rode him [to victory]."

Morrison continued to flirt with stardom as the season wore on. In a late-February game, he scored 26 points, all in the second half, to help Charlotte rally from a 17-point deficit and beat the Minnesota Timberwolves 100–95. Despite these outstanding individual performances, the Bobcats ended the year with a 33–49 record. After the uninspiring finish, Bobcats management fired Bickerstaff.

Before the 2007–08 season, the Bobcats introduced Sam Vincent, a former assistant coach with the Dallas Mavericks, as their new head coach. The organization hoped the young coach would connect with the Bobcats' young players. Charlotte continued its dealings by acquiring versatile forward Jermareo Davidson and clutch shooting guard Jason Richardson in a trade. Jordan was optimistic that Richardson would provide experienced leadership on the court. "We wanted a veteran player that we

felt could be a go-to player and create his own shots," he said. After defeating the Milwaukee Bucks and the Miami Heat for their first-ever 2–0 start, the Bobcats kept winning and went 6–4 over their first 10 contests.

However, then the team went into a tailspin. In mid-December, the Bobcats tried shuffling their roster, trading Brezec and Herrmann to the Pistons for 6-foot-10 and 250-pound center Nazr Mohammed. "Nazr brings the type of big body, experience, and athleticism that we have been looking to add to our team," said Bobcats general manager Rod Higgins. Despite Mohammed's superb inside defense and physical rebounding, the Bobcats remained far from playoff contention, finishing their fourth season a disappointing 32–50.

Next, the Bobcats exchanged youth for experience by firing Vincent and hiring longtime NBA coach Larry Brown. He had enjoyed success virtually everywhere he went, and his career reached its pinnacle when his Detroit Pistons became NBA champions in 2004. "I think you guys know Larry Brown, you know his history as a coach," Jordan told reporters. "He's from North Carolina. He went to the University of North Carolina, has family here. He's looking forward to coming back, and I'm very happy I could bring him back."

DEREK ANDERSON

OVERTIME TIMES THREE

On December 29, 2006, guard Kobe Bryant and the mighty Los Angeles Lakers rode into Charlotte, which was not good news for the Bobcats, who were in a three-game losing rut. The Bobcats battled hard, though, and with 43 seconds left in regulation, forward Gerald Wallace hit a shot plus a free throw to tie the game and send it into overtime. In the first overtime, with five seconds remaining, Bobcats guard Raymond Felton had a chance to put the game away but missed two potential game-winning shots. Another overtime passed without a winner. In the third overtime, with just over a minute left on the clock, Bobcats guard Derek Anderson was in the midst of launching a three-pointer when Bryant fouled him. Anderson hit all three of his foul shots to give the Bobcats a 129–124 lead. Thirty-five seconds later, Anderson stepped in front of a charging Bryant, forcing the Lakers superstar to foul out and helping preserve an unlikely 133–124 Bobcats victory. "Coach [Bickerstaff] has been on us, telling us to give a better show to the home fans," Wallace said. "I think it sunk in."

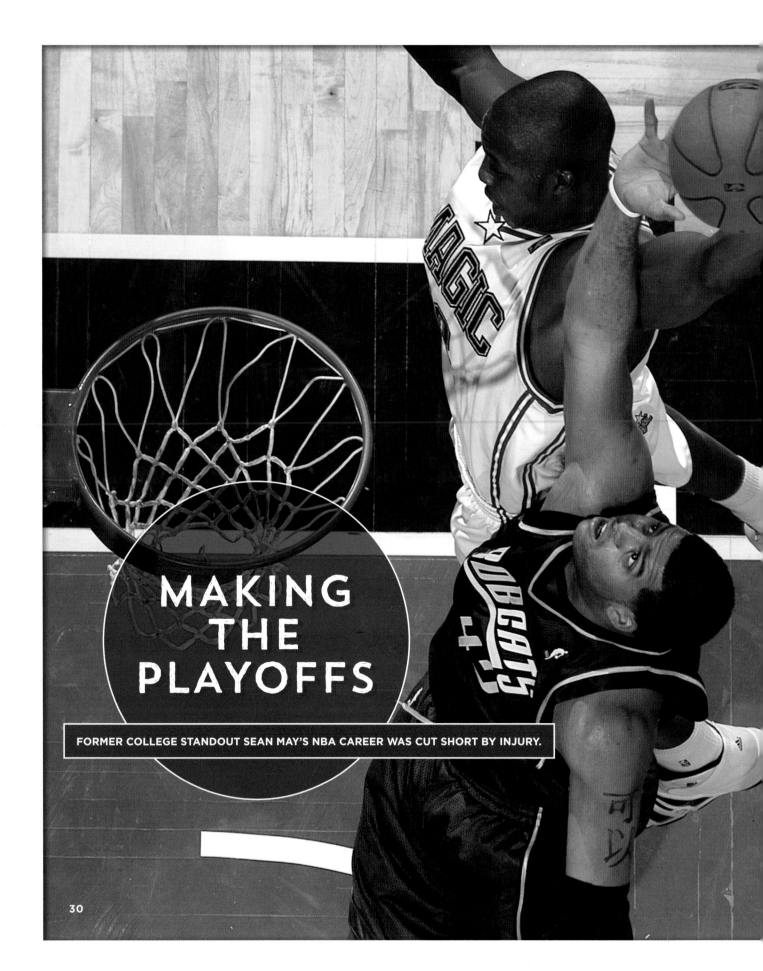

MAKING THE PLAYOFFS

FORMER COLLEGE STANDOUT SEAN MAY'S NBA CAREER WAS CUT SHORT BY INJURY.

Charlotte used the ninth overall pick in the 2008 NBA Draft to add University of Texas guard D. J. Augustin, known for his scrappy defensive skills and quick hands. Also chosen in the first round was French center Alexis Ajinca. A month later, the Bobcats signed Okafor, the face of the franchise, to a 6-year, $72-million contract. "It is exciting to enter the season with a Hall of Fame coach and teammates who are committed to winning," Okafor said.

Despite Okafor's optimism, Brown's leadership, and the urging of the Charlotte faithful, the Bobcats continued to struggle and started the 2008–09 campaign 5–11. The Bobcats made some roster changes in an effort to strengthen the lineup. Charlotte traded Richardson to the Phoenix Suns for versatile forward Boris Diaw and the defensive talents of guards Raja Bell and Sean Singletary,

THE CARDIAC CATS

In January 2008, the Bobcats became the "Cardiac Cats" to their fans as they earned some heart-stopping victories and suffered some wrenching defeats. On January 9, in Boston, the Bobcats upset the eventual NBA-champion Celtics 95–83. Two days later, Charlotte battled LeBron James and the Cleveland Cavaliers. With three-tenths of a second left in regulation, Bobcats guard Raymond Felton drilled a three-pointer from the top of the key to send the game into overtime. The contest went into a second overtime before the Cavaliers finally prevailed 113–106. The next night, the Bobcats took the Detroit Pistons into an overtime session in which the lead changed hands six times before Detroit finally won 103–100. And the best game may have occurred on January 16 against the Orlando Magic, when the Bobcats rallied from a 19-point third-quarter deficit behind forward Gerald Wallace's 36 points and 14 rebounds. Guard Jason Richardson had 13 points in the fourth quarter alone to put Charlotte ahead for good in a 99–93 triumph. "That's a big one for us," Richardson said. "It shows a lot of growth."

33

and then traded the Dallas Mavericks for center DeSagana Diop. "DeSagana is the type of player that has a natural athletic ability to block shots, rebound, and defend," noted Higgins.

From mid-February to early April, Charlotte went 16–12 and crept into playoff contention, thanks in large part to Okafor's low-post defense and the poise and scoring of Augustin. The most important driving force, however, might have been Wallace, who led the team in scoring in 10 games during March. On March 31, Charlotte topped the Lakers, completing a season sweep of Los Angeles and giving the Bobcats their franchise-record 34th win. In the end, Charlotte fell just short of the playoffs with a 35–47 mark.

Before the start of the 2009–10 season, Charlotte made a major move, trading Okafor to New Orleans for 7-foot-1 center Tyson Chandler. Although fans were sad to see Okafor go, Chandler's shot-blocking ability helped Charlotte continue to improve. After the club made a trade in November to obtain fiery, high-scoring forward Stephen Jackson,

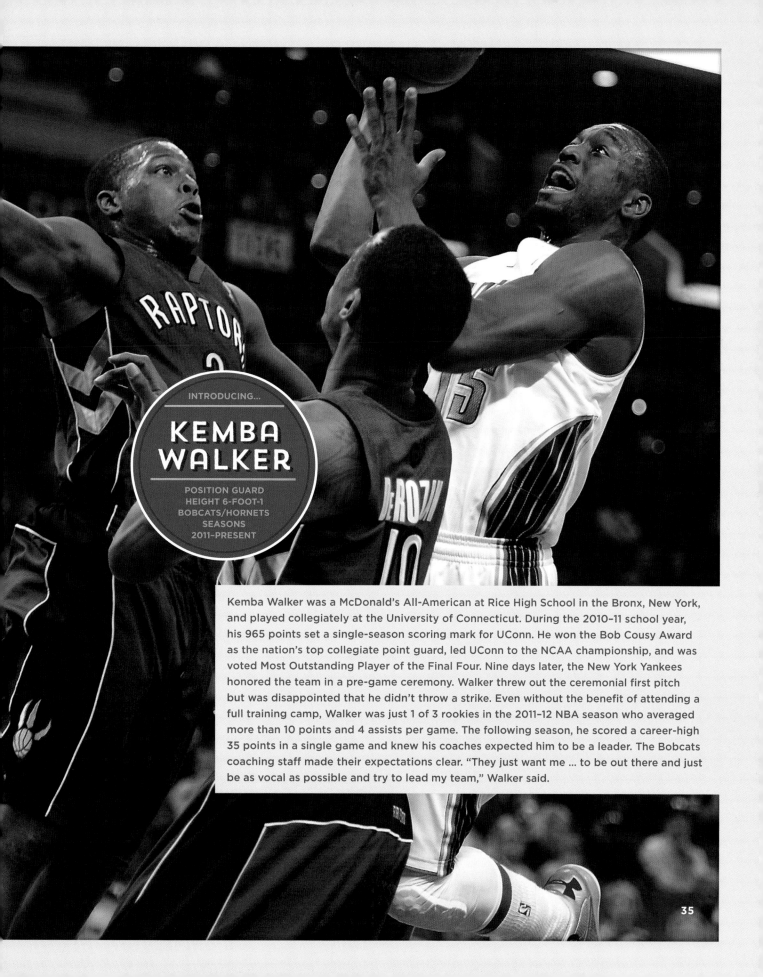

INTRODUCING...

KEMBA WALKER

POSITION GUARD
HEIGHT 6-FOOT-1
BOBCATS/HORNETS
SEASONS
2011–PRESENT

Kemba Walker was a McDonald's All-American at Rice High School in the Bronx, New York, and played collegiately at the University of Connecticut. During the 2010–11 school year, his 965 points set a single-season scoring mark for UConn. He won the Bob Cousy Award as the nation's top collegiate point guard, led UConn to the NCAA championship, and was voted Most Outstanding Player of the Final Four. Nine days later, the New York Yankees honored the team in a pre-game ceremony. Walker threw out the ceremonial first pitch but was disappointed that he didn't throw a strike. Even without the benefit of attending a full training camp, Walker was just 1 of 3 rookies in the 2011–12 NBA season who averaged more than 10 points and 4 assists per game. The following season, he scored a career-high 35 points in a single game and knew his coaches expected him to be a leader. The Bobcats coaching staff made their expectations clear. "They just want me ... to be out there and just be as vocal as possible and try to lead my team," Walker said.

the Bobcats really hit their stride, winning 9 of 10 games during a stretch in January. With Brown overseeing these new acquisitions and such reliable standouts as Felton and Wallace, Charlotte climbed above the .500 mark by midseason, finishing the year 44–38 and making the playoffs for the first time. The team was especially successful at home, riding the enthusiasm of Bobcats fans to a stellar 31–10 mark in Time Warner Cable Arena.

One key to their success was the NBA's best defense, as the Bobcats gave up 93.8 points per game. The flip side was a scoring-challenged offense, and Charlotte was ahead of only Detroit and New Jersey with an average of 95.3 points per game and trailing league-leading Phoenix by 15 points. Unfortunately, the Bobcats couldn't continue their momentum in the postseason, dropping all four games to the second-seeded Orlando Magic.

By that time, Johnson had sold Jordan majority rights to the team. The move made Jordan the first former player to become a franchise owner. "Purchasing the Bobcats is the culmination of my post-playing career goal of becoming the majority owner of an NBA franchise," Jordan said.

IN 2009–10, GERALD WALLACE WAS NAMED TO THE NBA ALL-DEFENSIVE FIRST TEAM.

NAZR MOHAMMED WARMED UP FOR CHARLOTTE'S PLAYOFF RUN IN HIS FIRST SEASON THERE.

A PERENNIAL LEADER, RAYMOND FELTON TOOK THE 'CATS TO NEW HEIGHTS IN THE LATE 2000s.

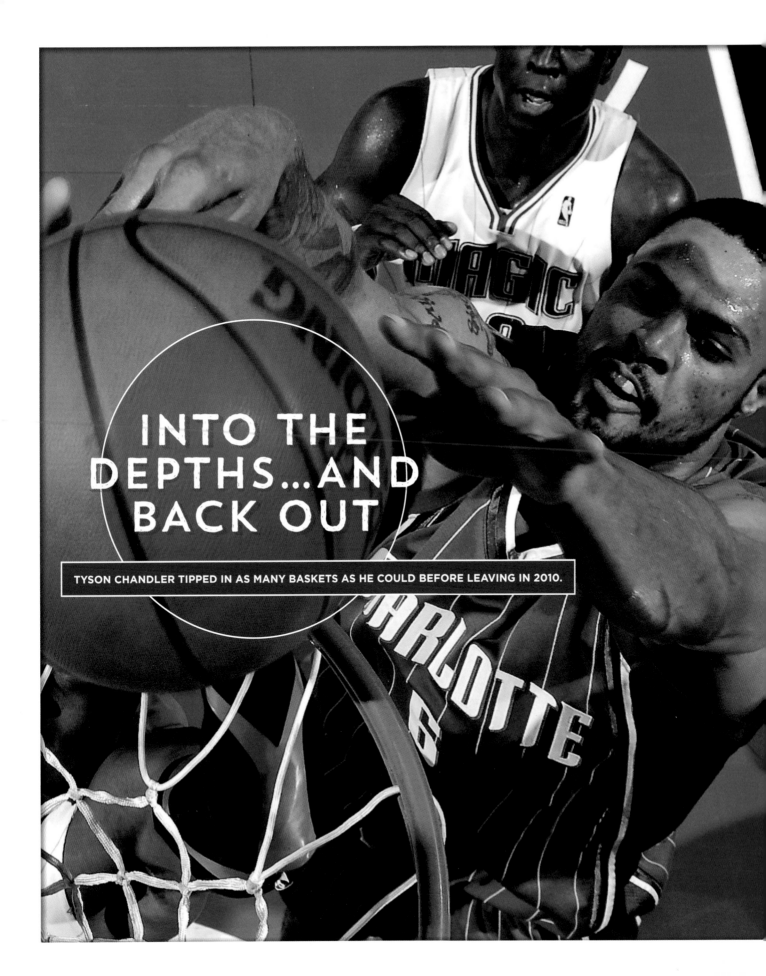

INTO THE DEPTHS...AND BACK OUT

TYSON CHANDLER TIPPED IN AS MANY BASKETS AS HE COULD BEFORE LEAVING IN 2010.

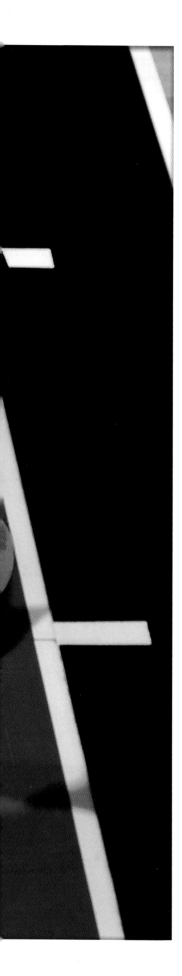

I t seemed to many fans as though Charlotte had turned the corner. Unfortunately, several factors combined to deflate their enthusiasm in the 2010–11 season. The team had traded away its draft picks and lost what would have been its first choice to the Denver Nuggets for the rights to Ajinca, who averaged just two points in limited action before being traded. After Felton left as a free agent, the team stumbled to a 9–19 start. Paul Silas then replaced Brown as head coach. Later in the season, Charlotte traded Wallace and Mohammed, and Jackson was injured soon afterward. The team struggled to a 34–48 mark—three games away from qualifying for the playoffs. In the 2011 NBA Draft, the Bobcats used their pair of top-10 picks on Congolese shot-blocking center Bismack Biyombo and University of Connecticut guard Kemba Walker. But no one could have foreseen what was about to happen.

AMIDST CHARLOTTE'S DISMAL 2011-12, GUARD GERALD HENDERSON HAD SEVERAL CAREER HIGHS.

A dispute between NBA owners and players delayed the start of the season and deprived the Bobcats—as well as every other team—of the practice time and exhibition games they needed. Nevertheless, Charlotte opened the shortened 2011–12 season with a thrilling 96–95 win over Milwaukee the day after Christmas, then dropped a one-point decision to the powerful Heat. Losing streaks of four and six games apiece set the table for a month-long dry spell between January 14 and February 17, when the Bobcats dropped 16 in a row. The lowest point was a 112–68 beat down in Portland's Rose Garden on February 1.

The worst was yet to come. After defeating Toronto 107–103 on March 17 for its 7th victory

(against 36 losses at that point), the team equaled its previous 16-game losing streak against Boston on April 15 and went on to drop the season's final 7 games to finish with the lowest-ever winning percentage in NBA history. Silas was fired.

The team's ill fortunes continued in the 2012 NBA Draft. According to the NBA Draft lottery system, the Bobcats had the best odds of securing the top pick. That would have netted them University of Kentucky freshman Anthony Davis, whom the Associated Press had named as the college basketball Player of

MICHAEL JORDAN

Michael Jordan's brilliant moves on the court haven't always translated to off-court success. He served as president of basketball operations with the Washington Wizards when he retired from the game, but was fired in 2003 for a number of questionable personnel decisions. Jordan came under fire for making similar judgment calls (such as drafting Adam Morrison) when he joined the Bobcats a decade later. Jordan's tenure reached rock bottom in 2011–12. "As a player, Jordan orchestrated the greatest season in NBA history," said ESPN writer Ryan McGee. "As an executive, he now owns the worst." Charlotte fans even booed him during the team's final home game that season. But there were signs that Jordan was turning over a new leaf and realizing he needed help; in June 2011, he hired Rich Cho as general manager, giving him full authority to reshape the Bobcats' roster. As BleacherReport.com basketball columnist Conner Boyd noted, "Just the mere fact that Jordan was willing to take to the passenger seat, if only partially, is proof that he is maturing as an owner, and is realizing that he can't build a team on his own."

FORWARD MICHAEL KIDD-GILCHRIST MADE THE NBA ALL-ROOKIE SECOND TEAM IN 2012–13.

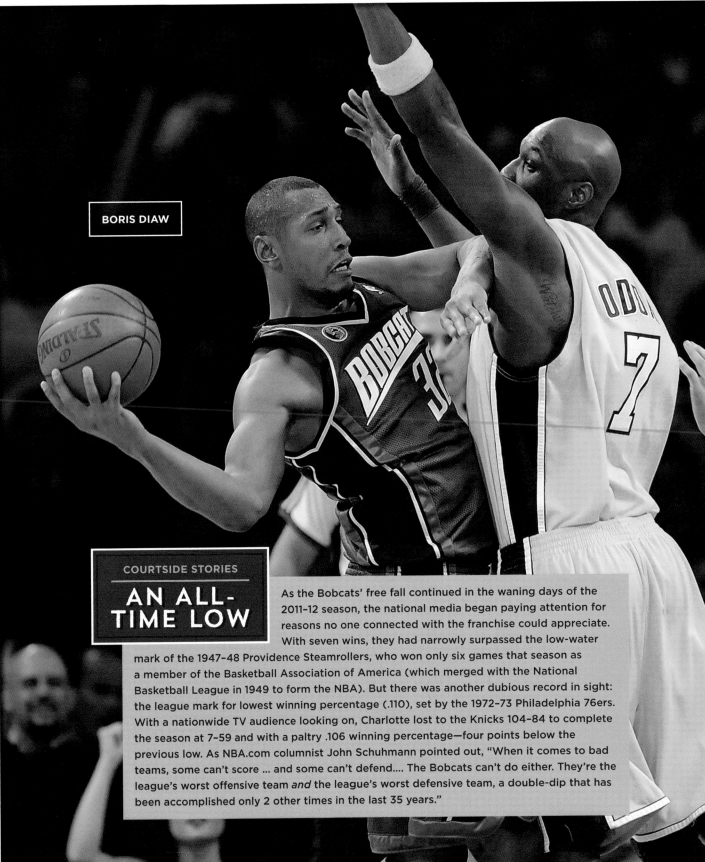

BORIS DIAW

COURTSIDE STORIES

AN ALL-TIME LOW

As the Bobcats' free fall continued in the waning days of the 2011–12 season, the national media began paying attention for reasons no one connected with the franchise could appreciate. With seven wins, they had narrowly surpassed the low-water mark of the 1947–48 Providence Steamrollers, who won only six games that season as a member of the Basketball Association of America (which merged with the National Basketball League in 1949 to form the NBA). But there was another dubious record in sight: the league mark for lowest winning percentage (.110), set by the 1972–73 Philadelphia 76ers. With a nationwide TV audience looking on, Charlotte lost to the Knicks 104–84 to complete the season at 7–59 and with a paltry .106 winning percentage—four points below the previous low. As NBA.com columnist John Schuhmann pointed out, "When it comes to bad teams, some can't score … and some can't defend…. The Bobcats can't do either. They're the league's worst offensive team *and* the league's worst defensive team, a double-dip that has been accomplished only 2 other times in the last 35 years."

the Year. But the Bobcats wound up with the second pick, which they used to select Davis's teammate Michael Kidd-Gilchrist. While some questioned why the offensively challenged Bobcats would choose a player who averaged only 12 points per game, general manager Rich Cho focused on Kidd-Gilchrist's overall appeal. Identifying him as a "winner" and "an ultra-competitor," Cho explained, "Out of the 17 years I've been in the NBA and involved with draft interviews and draft dinners, he's in the top 5 as far as that goes." The team drafted Vanderbilt University forward Jeffery Taylor, whom many observers considered a first-round talent, in the second round.

Charlotte also acquired veteran guard Ben Gordon to provide depth and three-point shooting and gained a future first-round draft pick in a trade with Detroit for Corey Maggette, one of the Bobcats' top scorers during the previous season. The team looked to Mike Dunlap, who had led Metropolitan State University of Denver to a pair of National Collegiate Athletic Association (NCAA) Division II national titles, to provide new leadership in the head coaching position.

nergized by all the new blood, Charlotte broke the previous season's losing streak by edging the Indiana Pacers 90–89 to open the 2012–13 season. When the Cats matched their previous season's 7-win total on November 24, it was the high-water mark, as they immediately launched an 18-game losing streak. After the season, Dunlap was replaced by Steve Clifford, who had 13 years of NBA experience as an assistant coach with 4 different teams. "Steve

is the type of guy who can coach young teams that are rebuilding, teams on the verge of the playoffs, and experienced teams," said Jeff Van Gundy, under whom Clifford had served for several years.

Clifford wasn't the only new name in Charlotte. In May 2013, Jordan announced that the team would return to its roots as Hornets in 2014–15, after New Orleans decided to change its name from Hornets to Pelicans. Many fans, especially those who had fond memories of the original Hornets, applauded the move. A Charlotte teacher named Scott Kent had a typical reaction. "[The Hornets] were given a name that represented our community, and that's really the big thing for me," Kent said. "Charlotte would be the hive, and the people would be the Hornets."

With the return of the team's "natural" nickname, "Back the Buzz" became the new catchphrase. Fittingly, the team turned in a buzzworthy 2013–14 season. Led by center Al Jefferson's 21.8 points and 10.8 rebounds per game, Charlotte went 43–39 and made the playoffs before getting swept in the first round by the Heat. Fans believed the team's fortunes had finally turned. On May 20, 2014, the franchise officially became the Charlotte Hornets once again and took back its 1988–2002 history and records from the Pelicans. Everyone connected with the team— front office, fans, players—hoped that other NBA teams would fear the hornets' nest in Charlotte, just as Cornwallis had more than two centuries before.

INDEX

WITHDRAWN